The Co-Creation Formula: How to Co-Create Your Life With The Universe

© Ramin Sultanov, 2022

Introduction

This book is the best gift for yourself and your loved one.

I might not have been able to write this book and share everything in it with you - it would have cost me a lot of effort, but my Higher Self easily carried out this work.

Proven techniques aimed at increasing awareness and achieving desired results will surprise you once you start using them.

Most of the work is already done for you and all that's left for you to do is follow simple instructions.

I believe that these methods work because without them, I would not be where I am right now.

Now, it's your turn to start changing your life for the better.

Who is this book for?

For those who feel that their life could have turned out differently, better than it is right now.

For those who feel that something is missing.

For those who feel the courage to create, but don't know where to start.

For those who are searching for themselves and want to find answers.

Why did I write this book?

I sincerely believe in the existence of our souls and that only in the harmony of soul, body, and mind, we can find peace and happiness.

I consider it my duty to share this knowledge and techniques so that more people could change their lives and fulfill their calling and as a result influence the lives of others as well. This book will change your life once and forever.

My book is intended to open your eyes, and bring you more awareness and happiness.

You have the right not to believe me, but once you put it all into practice, you will see how the formula simply works. I know that people always want proof, real examples. I don't like to prove anything to anyone. But I am that real example, the living proof.

I am an ordinary person, not better or worse than any of you. I was born in Baku, Azerbaijan. Since childhood, I wanted to create something amazing, something interesting. I have always been inspired by writers, poets, athletes, singers, actors, architects, musicians, scientists, political and public figures, philosophers, mathematicians - everyone who changed the world, who had the courage to bring something of their own into this world. That's exactly what I wanted to do.

My family has suffered a lot. I thought the world was unfair to me. I was very little, 4, maybe 5 years old, when my family was attacked and threatened by a special police unit, my dad and uncle were beaten, money and valuables were taken away, our apartment was put in their name, they even took tape recorders and clothes. I remember one of those times, when they knocked on our door, cursing, and threatening us, I grabbed a small knife and waited for them at the front door. "If only they try to enter!" thought little Ramin. We were desperate, but thanks to my grandmother Sumara (my dad's mom), miraculously we were able to get the apartment back. Somehow, we recovered, but only on the surface. Now I understand that the psychological trauma remained with all of us forever. It was underlying all our future decisions.

Nevertheless, I managed to answer the main question for myself: do I feel self-pity and struggle, blaming everyone around me, or do I take life into my own hands and try, at least, to do something to improve my situation? I chose the latter.

Years later, I realized that I made the right choice.

Our story

When Firuza and I met at the end of 2017, we immediately started planning our future together.

It was the beginning of 2018 when we launched our first business. That summer we quit our corporate jobs and devoted ourselves entirely to our new venture. Every day we'd work from the co-working space, staying late, sometimes until midnight, and working 16 hours a day.

It was not easy, but we were unstoppable. Neither our parents nor friends supported us. This gave us a push, it made us stronger and we relied solely on ourselves and each other.

We got married in 2019 and for our honeymoon, we traveled to places like Bali, Kuala Lumpur, Cappadocia, etc.

In January 2020, we returned to Baku and continued exploring the topic of mindset - this quest started during our trip. Meditation, visualization, and manifestation have since become our best friends.

We used to wake up at 4:30 am to work on our business and mindset, attend courses and read. The same year, we sent out our startup project applications to various organizations in Europe and got invited to move there to launch our business.

In April 2021 we moved to Portugal.

In 2022 we launched our startup - Floovly.

25A +50 + 25B

What is 25A+50+25B about?

This formula came to me while Firuza (my wife) and I were at the beach in early July 2022. We sunbathed, talked, expressed gratitude for our beautiful life, and fantasized about how we would make the world more conscious and give people opportunities to become better, happier, and more mindful. We swam in the ocean and as we were about to leave, I suddenly told Firuza, "25+50+25". She looked at me confused and didn't understand what I meant. I didn't understand it either, but I began elaborating on it to her as if I'd known about it for many years. It just struck me.

Through this formula, I am going to tell you how to achieve anything you want if you truly desire it with all your heart. I later modified the formula a little: the first 25 to 25A and the second 25 to 25B to make it clear that 25A is the first part of our task, then comes the 50 of the

Universe, and only after that do we implement our second part, 25B.

I received this formula when I sincerely asked the Universe to show me ways to convey to people that they can easily achieve anything they dream about, if only they desire it with all their heart.

"What if I don't desire it with all my heart, what then?", you may ask. Then you don't need the fulfillment of these desires and goals, they are not yours, they were imposed on you. "How is that possible?", you might wonder.

Our society, the media, our parents, schools, universities, the environment, and the entire system influences us in one way or another. In some cases, this happens intentionally, to impact how and what decisions we make. In some cases, this happens unintentionally, nevertheless, we end up believing that we want certain things. The truth is, we don't want them, we were sold this idea. Through TV, authorities, celebrities, some dogmas, religion, etc.

I feel like the formula 25A + 50 + 25B was put into my mind. It was sudden and unexpected. I realize that now my main mission is to show everyone how easy it is to create the life they dream about. And to do this, they don't need to hustle, have any outstanding abilities, connections or be extra smart (see chapter "Beliefs and Fears")

The only requirement is to be mindful. This can be easily mastered if you understand why you want to create life on your terms, rather than expecting someone else to do it for you. People will gladly create a life for you, but not the one you dream of. If you don't serve yourself, you will serve others and their dreams. This formula, I would even call it a revelation, changed my life, our life with Firuza. Finally, everything makes sense now.

All you need is to follow this simple formula.

25A - your intention. You declare what you desire. You can do this by writing down your goals, wishes, and desires.

50 - the response from the Universe. The Universe reacts to your intentions and shows you the way.

25B - your actions. After receiving the signs from the Universe, it's your turn to take specific actions.

Unlike the standard and generally accepted approach where you immediately act or think and then act, in the case of 25A + 50 + 25B, you are guaranteed to achieve what you desire if you properly recognize the signs of the Universe.

You see, as our souls come here (to Earth) with the purpose of learning our lessons and becoming closer to our Higher self, you must understand what you truly want, what you truly need, and what is truly important to you. If the desire isn't truly yours, if it's influenced by someone or something from the external world, you shouldn't pursue it. Your mind will tell you one thing, but it's quite different when your soul starts whispering.

Our mission, as human beings, is to listen to the voice of our soul and recognize its signals, this is the only way we will learn our lessons and attain our goals. To hear the voice of our soul, we need to be mindful and conscious. And to stop trying to break into the wrong doors!

Of course, you could still manage to walk the path that's not truly yours. You might even think that since you're on this path, that you're on the right path but unfortunately, that's not the case. If there were no signs from the Universe leading you through this path, it was meant for you.

A valuable trait that you must have in order to catch the signals of your soul, rather than your mind, is the ability to surrender, knowing that the Universe will provide everything for you at the right time, in the best possible way. We are the co-creators of our life, not the sole creators. Therefore, we are responsible for 50% of the process, the Universe takes care of the other 50%. We create together with the Universe. We divide 50% of our work into 2 parts, this is very important. We won't be able to perform the entire 50% of our work in one go. The Universe has that kind of power to do it, but we don't. It is extremely important to follow the sequence of the steps. Don't skip, don't swap.

The first step (25A) in the co-creation formula is creating the vision of your life (I recommend referring to the **Future Self exercise,** which I will discuss later in the book). This is where you set your intentions.

At this point, your goal is to visualize the life you desire. You need to be clear and intentional when deciding what kind of life you desire. Write down your goals, wishes, desires, and intentions.

You can visualize anything: who you are, where you live, whom you live with, how you live, who surrounds you, what you do and how you enjoy what you do, who your friends are, your environment, how you change the world for the better, the things you create that benefit the Universe, people, souls (refer to the **Visualization exercise** further in the book).

For instance, Firuza and I visualized our life in a place where we feel comfortable, where we feel valued, where people have a certain attitude towards each other, where we can achieve our goals on our own, and where society does not have certain stereotypes. We envisioned the life that we want to live every day: visualized how we are maximizing our potential, creating interesting projects that benefit people, and the planet. At the same time, while visualizing we focused on the feelings we would experience in that desired future - this is the only way to complete step one and move on to the second part of the formula.

In life, from the very first days, we are in constant search for ourselves, we try different activities, and jobs and we look for our purpose in the outside world. We keep trying to implement step 3 without undertaking the first two steps. Most people don't succeed because everything in our world comes in sequences. You have to keep in mind that timing is key, and everything happens at the perfect time. Right now, you may not comprehend what I mean, but very soon you will realize that the formula 25A + 50 + 25B is the key to your success, the road that will lead you to the life you dream about faster than anything else. Start creating your new reality, a life that brings you joy and fulfillment!

At this point (step 1), you need to learn to visualize and at the same time, to feel the emotions of your desired future. This way, you will be able to program your body and your mind to the new reality, where you have what you desire, it's already yours.

It is crucial not only to visualize your intention but to feel it with every cell of your body - this signifies that we truly and deeply desire it. Now it's time to move to the second step.

The second step (50) is when the Universe (the Energy of the Cosmos, God) based on our intentions, thoughts, and emotions, responds by leading us and opening necessary doors. All events and situations align for us to receive our desires. Incredible and unbelievable things start to take place, the right people appear out of nowhere, and events unfold in favorable ways - everything starts happening for us. It might seem like the entire world is ready to do anything to make you happy. Trust me, it's not an illusion.

This is how the Universe performs its part (50). The Universe delivers based on your order.

The Universe will help you in every possible way. New doors will open and fascinating opportunities will emerge.

At some point you might notice that you're given not what you precisely wished for - there is a very important message here. This is like a test from the Universe, to check if you truly and deeply desire what you visualized in the first step. If you accept the alternative, you are in trouble. You have strayed off course.

You will need to remind yourself of your true desire and stop believing that a bird in the hand is worth two in the bush. This is not your bird. This is the rational mind convincing you of the advantages of something mediocre and readily available, over something worthy, beautiful, but "difficult" to attain. It is unreachable for your rational mind, not you. Your rational mind doesn't have the guts to do something daring! It's always playing safe!

Do you know why? Because of the old programs deeply rooted in our subconscious mind. Since childhood, we've been fed with negative programs and beliefs that don't serve our purpose in life. We have forgotten our true selves, and who we truly are, we've forgotten our mission in life. Prejudices and fears that we live by, keep us from creating truly wonderful things. But there is always a way out.

In the second step of the formula, the Universe suggests ideas and implementation plans. At this stage, we are given everything we need to receive our desired outcome.

However, we live in the physical world, and therefore, we need to take life into our own hands and finish the process we initiated. The remaining step – our 25% (25B).

Sometimes at stage 50, when the Universe is searching for ways, it doesn't show you anything. It means that you are not supposed to do anything about this goal right now. Maybe the timing isn't right. If and when the time is right, the Universe will let you know. At this point, your task is to pick up the signals, which might not always be obvious. That's the reason why you need to learn to be mindful and conscious. If you live unconsciously, you will not be able to spot the signs. You will try to break in and enter doors that are not yours, you will not follow your true path which is fraught with consequences. At best you will be unhappy and ignore the voice of your soul, which in turn will lead to serious consequences at work, in business, and your personal life.

If at this stage (50) you don't notice a positive response to your request then you shouldn't proceed to 25B. Even if you deeply desire it. If you didn't receive permission from the Universe, then it's better not to act upon it.

The third step (25B) is when we complete the process we initiated in the first step, which was also supported by the Universe in the second step. This step is about action. Once the Universe sends us the right people, events, and situations, the ideas will start flooding our mind and we can then act upon these ideas. Our actions are our second 25% of the task - the 25B.

Remember, only after you see all the possibilities presented by the Universe you can undertake action.

At this stage, you have everything you need to take the next steps toward your goal:

You have a vision of what you desire from step 1

You have ideas about how to implement and what tools to use from step 2

Now, you must simply take action.

At this point, it is very easy to take the last steps toward your goal since you already know what and how to implement it.

When can you use the formula 25A +50+25B?

Whenever you want to achieve something. For instance, if you want to get accepted to a specific university, all you need to do is visualize it in your mind (25A) and then wait for signs from the Universe (50). Only when you receive the sign, take the action (25B). This way you will certainly succeed. Most people don't get what they want because they push too hard. It doesn't work that way.

25A implies that you visualize your desired outcome in your mind without taking any action, although at times you can take little steps, I'll give you an example next.

You want to take a trip. Visualize how awesome and fun the vacation is, the places you visit, and the emotions you feel. Then wait for signs from the Universe. At this stage, you can also start checking airplane tickets and hotels, for example. Thus, declaring your desire and expressing your intention to take this trip. Then, if the timing is right, the Universe will give you the signs.

Do not buy anything until there is a positive response from the Universe during the second stage. If there is a negative response or you don't see a response, it's best to cancel the trip at this time or maybe to this specific destination. Perhaps later, you might be able to travel there. If so, you will definitely notice the signs. If at step 50 you don't see the sign or you receive a negative response, it means the Universe doesn't approve of your decision and it's not the best possibility for you right now.

If you rebel and ignore the signs of the Universe, you can expect obstacles: from harmless nuisances to big challenges.

The formula 25A+50+25B in action

At the beginning of 2021, Firuza and I received offers from a few European countries inviting us to relocate and launch our business project (startup) in Europe. We decided to accept one of the invites and relocate to Portugal.

Before moving to Portugal, we wanted to take a trip to Dubai (United Arab Emirates). We started planning the trip but realized there were no direct flights or only flights with 10-hour layovers. That certainly didn't fit into our idea of taking a luxury vacation. First, this upset us, but then we decided that if direct flights appeared before a certain date, then we'd take the trip. The departure time should be convenient and of course, it should be a direct Baku-Dubai flight. "If there are no flights matching these criteria, then we are not supposed to travel there. At least not now", we thought.

We surrendered. After a couple of days, we read the news announcing that direct flights to Dubai were operating again and we realized that this was a sign from the Universe.

Everything happened in the best possible way for us and at the right time. All of this is simply because we had faith - the Universe is on our side and it knows what's best for us. The important lesson here is not only that the formula 25A + 50 + 25B worked, but that you need to learn to trust the Universe and surrender, loosening your grip on the situation.

Everything will resolve itself in a way that you couldn't have imagined. We truly enjoyed these two weeks in Dubai and it was one of the best trips we've ever taken.

Another example of the formula in action is when I signed up for surfing lessons. For a while, I kept thinking about whether I should try it or not. One of those days, an acquaintance, whom I met at a coffee shop, told me that he signed up for surfing classes and that it was very convenient, they picked you up and dropped you off, and equipment and lunch were included too. This sounded lucrative so I immediately signed up for five lessons in a row. I was exhausted after each class. Because as I can see looking back now, I did not follow the 25A + 50 + 25B formula. I was seduced by the rational benefit of this opportunity, the fact that they'd pick me up, drop me off, and provide lunch seemed like a good deal. And of course, it was a good deal indeed, but firstly, I had to listen to the voice of my soul, what was it telling me? This doesn't mean that surfing is not my thing at all, but I signed up for classes without considering the 25A + 50 + 25B formula. If I had done it according to the formula, there wouldn't have been a shadow of a doubt, there wouldn't have been so much exhaustion. Now that I look back, I realize there was actually an interesting sign from the Universe. The day after the first lesson we received an email with an invitation to present our startup project to the President of Portugal, which was scheduled for the next day in Lisbon. I was forced to reschedule the second surfing lesson so that Firuza and I could travel to Lisbon. We also had to come back to Algarve, to Lagos, on the same day, late at night, so that I wouldn't miss the second surfing lesson.

After those five surfing lessons, my entire palms were scratched from the friction with the surfboard, I could barely hold it by the fourth lesson. Now, I can clearly see that the situation turned out this way because I signed up for surfing classes at the wrong time. Timing is very important. You have to trust that you receive what you truly desire at the right time and in the best possible way. Funnily, there isn't a single photo of me surfing although the company arranged for a photographer to take everyone's photos. Everyone, except me, received their photos.

In the end, since I didn't follow the 25A+50+25B formula, I didn't enjoy surfing. I even got hit on the head with the surfboard a couple of times. These are the unpleasant consequences that can occur when you ignore the formula of co-creation, when you don't listen to the voice of your soul and only follow the rational mind.

Anyone, who's not following his true path is risking living a life without discovering himself and his potential. This is exactly why our souls came to Earth. The consequences of not following our path or following not our truest path could be very serious.

In addition to the fact that the formula 25A + 50 + 25B helps you attain any goal and fulfill any desire, it serves as a guide, it's like a compass that shows us the right way. Thanks to this formula, you will follow a path that's aligned with your true purpose.

The Universe will nudge you in every possible way when you're about to take the wrong path. Thanks to the formula, you will no longer be envious of others because you'll come to realize that everyone is meant to follow their own path. You will stop pointing fingers and this in turn will positively affect your entire life. All the answers are within us. As soon as you grasp this you will become more self-aware, you'll understand those around you, and discover your purpose. All the desires that don't belong to you will disappear. You will keep only what's truly yours.

I will give you another great example of how the formula has worked out for me in the past. As soon as we moved to Portugal in April 2021, we started looking for an apartment to rent. It was important for us to find an apartment with an annual contract since we needed the contract as part of our residency application. We couldn't find anything matching our needs in Lisbon.

At that point, we had no idea that eventually we'll move to the very south of Portugal, to the Algarve. After many unsuccessful attempts to find an apartment in Lisbon, we started searching everywhere else around Portugal. The deadline was approaching but we still hadn't found an apartment. Staying at hotels for longer periods became very inconvenient. During this time we did one very important thing. We kept in mind the image of our perfect home - beautiful, cozy, and right by the ocean. We were performing the 25A, without realizing that we were actually following the formula.

Suddenly, we got contacted by a real estate agency and miraculously they had only one apartment that was available for exactly one year. Everything else was taken. At that time, we were staying in central Portugal and for the next two months, we had a few trips planned to Spain and Italy. Basically, we didn't have the time to visit the south of Portugal to view the apartment. The photos of the apartment were of poor quality and even when the agency sent us a video review we were still unsure. In the end, we signed the contract without physically viewing the apartment. We decided to trust the Universe and let it take care of us.

Imagine our surprise when, two months later, we arrived to the Algarve and moved into our new house - a large, cozy apartment, an 8-minute walk away from the beach and the ocean! The old town is 15-20 minutes away, it takes us 20-25 minutes to walk to our favorite cafes, restaurants, and the tennis court, where we play every week. The location is great and most importantly the area is very clean, cozy, and quiet.

Even during the summer season when Lagos is flooded with tourists, our area remains peaceful and calm, which is exactly what we wanted. The weather is wonderful too, it's sunny and warm and you can even swim in the ocean all year round.

The Universe, considered our request, our 25A, and provided the opportunity, the 50. We simply had faith and didn't look for other apartments. We trusted the Universe and proceeded to our 25B, signed the contract, and moved in.

Later that year, we will fully comprehend why we were destined to move to Portugal, to the Algarve, to Lagos, to live in this specific area, and even on this specific street.

Learn to surrender and let go of the situation. You will gain so much power once you realize that you don't need to control everything and everyone.

Here's another story to give you a better understanding of the positive effects of surrendering.

Last year Firuza and I decided to buy a drone. I am generally not a fan of photo/video equipment and I always say that photography is not my thing. But the very idea of using something new appealed to me.

A few days later we were by the pool and I decided to start the drone. Suddenly, while in the air an engine error occurred and the drone began to move farther and farther away, higher, and eventually disappeared into the unknown.

Naturally, we got very upset. The drone was bought a few days ago and now it was gone. Right at that moment, it started pouring rain. Despite that, we went searching for the drone, we looked all over the area where it could have possibly landed, but to no avail. I got angry and cursed, but obviously, this didn't solve the problem.

We contacted the manufacturer of the drone and explained what happened. They refused to do anything about it.

We decided that it is best to surrender and trust. "There must be a reason why this happened and we will soon realize it," we thought.

This is what happened next.

The manufacturer sent us a new drone and we found the old one.

A few days after the incident we got a knock on our door, it was our neighbors asking us to follow them to their house. As we reached their house, a guy came out and handed us our drone, all safe and sound. It turns out that our drone fell right in their garden. Looking back we ask ourselves: "what were the odds?"

Firstly, it was off-season and almost no one lived in the area around us (we were staying at a resort). Secondly, these neighbors stayed there only for a few days. What was the probability that our drone would have landed in their garden exactly during these few days?

Think about it, as soon as we let go of the situation, we received two drones.

We thanked the neighbors and decided to come back later and give them a gift. Unfortunately, they never received the gift. We stopped by their house every other day for almost two months and kept knocking, but no one was ever home. Seemed like they arrived for a couple of days just to return the drone to us.

Now you can clearly see the amazing events that can happen once you let go and surrender.

You will be even more surprised to hear the next story. You might think: "That's a miracle!" And I'll agree with you, our life is full of miracles. Only these miracles can happen to everyone and not just to a select few.

In the summer of 2021, we wanted to rent a car in Lisbon but it seemed impossible. Especially with an automatic transmission. We set the intention - we need a car, with an automatic transmission, as soon as possible and without providing a credit card. We don't use credit cards and car rental agencies almost always require credit cards, they don't accept debit or prepaid cards. Right at the time when we needed it the most, unexpectedly we managed to find a car with an automatic transmission for three months. We paid online, but we weren't sure what would happen when we picked up the car. If they didn't accept our debit card, we wouldn't have been able to receive a refund. Keep in mind that we paid the full amount for one month in advance. Once again, we were lucky - they accepted the debit card. This is not the end though, read what happens next.

We used the car for three months; we did a road trip around Portugal and Spain. Of course, by the time we had to return it, there were scratches and even a broken backlight glass. And yes, the car was not insured.

We realized that we would probably have to pay several thousand euros. At first, as usual, we got upset. But, as time went by, we let go of the situation and accepted what was to come. We told ourselves that whatever happens, happens for us and for our own good. If we'd have to pay thousands of euros then be it. It would only mean that for some reason this was necessary, that there was a hidden lesson.

The rental period ended and we drove to the agency to return the car. I held the following thought in my mind and visualized: I am leaving the agency happy and satisfied. I didn't know which specific outcome would make me happy, I simply let go of the situation and trusted the Universe.

What do you think happened next? The car got checked, and I was asked if it was insured. Obviously, they looked shocked as I told them that it wasn't. They made a few notes about the minor scratches but surprisingly didn't seem to notice the bigger ones. At this point, I was in complete disbelief myself and I asked them to take a look at the car one more time. They responded that there was no need to check again and that I was free to leave.

Did you anticipate such turn of events? My intention worked, and I left the agency happy and satisfied. I didn't pay a dime.

Events and Media

Using the formula 25A+50+25B, we were invited as speakers to present at events and conferences. Firuza and I had an image in our mind - to be invited to various events where we'd share our experience and story. That was our 25A. The next step was to wait for the 50 - the sign from the Universe. It did not take long. We started receiving invites to participate at various events. 25B – we attended and spoke at those events.

Firuza and I also wanted some press coverage for our startup. We held our intention, visualized it, and sent a few emails to some media channels. These were our 25A. At this stage, as I said, you can take small steps that require minor effort and energy. We then waited for an answer from the Universe (50).

Journalists began replying (it was the 50), and we even met with some of them - that was our 25B and shared our story, which was then published in magazines and newspapers.

The world is a mirror

Do you want to be treated with respect? Show respect first. Start treating everyone you encounter with respect.

If you want people to stop hurting or offending you, first try to recall the people you hurt or offended. Maybe you were rude to your mother or the postman, perhaps you hurt your children or employees/colleagues?

Think about it, you will certainly recall something. This is not the main takeaway though; we've all offended or hurt someone at some point in our lives. The key is to recognize this and stop repeating it. You will soon witness how the world, all of a sudden, starts treating you differently.

If you feel like you are not appreciated, that your work is not valued – think about the times you undervalued someone's work. The world is a mirror, it reflects to you exactly what you are. What you give into this world is what you receive back. This is how energy works.

If you surround yourself with negativity, if you complain about life – that's what you will get back. If you think positively, the world around you will begin to change, although it might not happen right away.

I'll give you a chance to object "How can I think positively when I have serious problems?" This is what I'd say to you, "There isn't a single problem, challenge, or situation in your life that you aren't equipped to handle. If this challenge appeared on your way, in my point of view, this can only mean one thing - you are capable of solving it." For some unknown reason, it was gifted to you. Any problems, as we call them, are sent our way so that we can go through the experience, learn our lessons and become more conscious and happier. This is why our souls come to Earth.

Accept that this is how the world is and don't try to change it. It is much better for you to adapt and witness how the world reflects and becomes a safer and happier place for you.

By focusing on the problem, you are sabotaging yourself and amplifying the negativity. You're facing a problem? Nobody says to ignore it, simply look at it from a different angle and realize that this problem is created for you. Be curious, start looking for solutions, and do your 25A, and the answer will come. The Universe will show you a direction and then you can perform the 25B, and take specific actions. Don't be upset! If there is a problem, there is a solution and this problem will only improve your life. Once you view the problem from a different angle, you will not only stop feeling upset, you'll actually be fascinated. Nothing is black and white, good or bad - the world is much more multifaceted than you might think. With your stream of positive thoughts, you'll handle any problem and things will fall into place magically.

You can create any kind of life you desire. All you have to do is believe in it. Human beings are very powerful. Don't say, "I'm just an ordinary person, I can't do this." Speak and feel as if you are capable of achieving anything. Being human in itself implies that we are intelligent enough to accomplish big goals. We have a mind that solves complex problems and comes up with ideas, we have a body, which guides us in the right direction, and we have a soul, where all the answers exist. It is crucial to learn to hear and listen to your inner self.

The Universe always supports you

There was a time, while living in Moscow when I tried to start a business, but back then I didn't give the Universe a chance to show me the right way.

I tried to start so many different projects, but none of them were born from within my heart. My mistake was that I was starting with 25B, which is supposed to be the second part of my task. I tried to start any business with anyone, just for the sake of making money.

What I had to do is start with 25A. I had to design a vision of what I wanted to create in my life and then I had to wait for the opportunities and signs from the Universe. Only after that, after having the ideas and implementation plans, I should have gone forward with 25B, the action. If I had followed this sequence, I would have certainly achieved my goals. But I didn't allow myself to hear my soul.

Since childhood, I have been very interested in sports, especially football. I watched it, played it, collected stickers, newspapers, and magazines, played computer games, and learned by heart the names of the players of the most popular teams. I could even recall the precise times specific players scored goals, although these games were played more than 20-30 years ago. That's the kind of football fan I was. Very often I thought about connecting my work with what I truly liked - football. This was my 25A, my intention. And the Universe performed its 50 and gave me a few chances.

One of them happened in 2010, at the time when I was studying for my university degree in Moscow and working at the same time. A classmate called me and said that his father is opening a bookmaker's office and needs a trustworthy person. I was told that this person should preferably love and be knowledgeable about football. I perfectly fit the description. I somehow managed to arrange my time and started working there as well. And I really enjoyed it. My job, although not easy, was interesting and I felt comfortable doing my work.

I was then given another opportunity. I saw an announcement - a sports TV channel was looking for football commentators. I had to pass some exams and submit an application. You could say that this was a dream come true - a job related to football and travel. The Universe presented an opportunity, gave me a sign, confirming that I was on the right track. But back then I was far from listening to the voice of my soul and didn't allow myself to try. I didn't apply for the position, justifying it with my busy schedule, studies, and two jobs. I told myself, "Everything is actually fine, I'm happy with my life, and I don't need this job."

Or maybe I was just afraid of failure? If you follow the formula, you will not be scared to move forward, because everything is quite simple. If the Universe hasn't answered yet, wait. If the answer is negative, don't take any action. If the answer is positive, go ahead. In all three cases, you won't be intimidated because you know how the co-creation formula works.

My mistake was that I didn't hear what my soul was telling me. This is exactly what I had dreamt about, my 25A. The Universe delivered the 50 and all I had to do was take action (25B). But I missed it all and took the wrong turn.

I had a chance to walk the path of my soul one more time. I signed up for acting classes in Moscow, which was around 2013-14. When I take classes, courses, and trainings, I am usually very disciplined. Everyone who knows me can confirm this, especially my wife Firuza. During these acting classes, I perfectly completed all of the required exercises and tasks, some of which had to be performed on the street, in the subway, and coffee shops. In order to become confident in public speaking I had to perform quite interesting and challenging tasks.

Here are some examples: I had to read poetry in the subway and in a coffee shop. I also had to go up to strangers, pretending to speak a non-existent language and get them to say their names. Another task required me to approach people on the street and find out their names, but I had to pretend to be mute and use non-verbal signs only.

I wasn't just the first to complete these exercises, I was also the fastest in the entire history of this acting school. As a result, one of our teachers offered me a public speaking job. At that time, I was already working in an office job and thought that the public speaking job didn't suit me. But then, I realized that I enjoyed speaking in public, I'm not afraid of the crowd and I'm very good at it. I also speak, write and express my thoughts in Russian language very well, so why not? "If it doesn't work out, oh well! But if it does, that would be amazing, I'd be doing something interesting instead of analyzing data in the office", I thought.

Guess what happened next? I became the most popular public speaker of all time. You haven't heard of me? Because I didn't.

The schedule didn't work for me and I rejected the offer. A while later, they invited me to another event but I missed it again, justifying that I didn't have the time, it wasn't my thing and that wasn't a serious job.

Who said it had to be serious? These are all our beliefs, and conditioning that we need to reprogram to start hearing the voice of our soul.

My dream was to speak publicly, these were my 25A. The Universe presented opportunities and options - the 50. All I had to do was take action - my 25B, which I missed because I wasn't sure if that was the right thing for me. But I wasn't sure because I wasn't aware of the formula. Luckily, now you are familiar with it.

How we moved to Europe based on the formula 25A+50+25B

We wanted to live and create in a place where our work is valued, and where people we meet are aligned with our values. We knew for sure that we don't belong in Azerbaijan. We felt most drawn to Europe.

But we had no idea how to relocate to Europe, where to set up our business, or where to live. We simply dreamed about it. We visualized our life in a beautiful place, we imagined ourselves enjoying life and the work we do, the location and our lifestyle, and the people surrounding us. We meditated and visualized our new life every single day.

This was our 25A and that's how the idea of our global startup was born. We applied to various organizations in Europe, had numerous calls, and exchanged hundreds of emails. As a result, we got accepted into several startup programs in Europe. We chose Portugal. We chose this country because we closely listened to the voice of our soul. As soon as we got the invitation we began preparing the documents that had to be presented at the embassy.

We found out that there was no embassy or consulate of Portugal in Azerbaijan, hence Firuza had to travel to Ankara (Turkey) to apply for the visa, and I had to travel to Moscow (Russia). Keep in mind that this is 2020 and the world is going through a pandemic, borders are closed, no one is allowed to travel to the EU. We would have spent a lot of time, money and undergone a lot of stress if not for the French Embassy in Baku (Azerbaijan). They helped us immensely and provided the visas directly in Baku. A huge thank you to them!

April 16, 2021 - the day we landed in Lisbon and almost cried tears of joy. That was the second part of our task, the 25B. The formula worked! 25A - we visualized our life in Europe, 50 - the Universe provided the opportunities and directions, everything from the idea of our startup to the relocation plan. 25B - we did what we had to do, we just took the flight.

Travel example

Firuza and I wanted to travel in the summer of 2022. We started planning different routes. We checked out various destinations - Berlin, Budapest, Vienna and other cities in Europe. But every time something just didn't feel right. We did our 25A, but before proceeding to 25B, before taking any action, we had to wait for the 50 from the Universe, the signs, ideas, plans. The sign didn't come. At first, we were upset, but then we consciously recognized that absolutely everything is within our power. If we believe that everything happens against us, then that's exactly what it's going to be. If we are certain that everything happens for us, then that's what we'll witness.

We decided to let go and surrender. This is a very useful tool or technique, call it whatever you like, but make sure you use it at all times.

We surrendered to the idea that maybe it's better for us not to travel right now. Remember, don't knock on doors that are closed, they're closed for your own good. This is not your path. You can, of course, eventually break in. But you'll end up disappointed at best.

Then one evening, all of a sudden I was reminded of my favorite waltz by Anthony Hopkins (Hollywood actor), performed by the wonderful conductor Andre Rieu.

I googled "concert program of Andre Rieu" and got a list of European cities where he'd be performing in 2022. A small Dutch town called Maastricht caught my eye. An open-air concert – an idea that delighted my soul. I told Firuza that I must fulfil this desire of my soul and we must travel to Maastricht for Andre Rieu's concert. We immediately began planning: hotels, flights and so on.

We thought that we might as well travel to nearby cities like Amsterdam, Bruges, Brussels, Lille, Paris and the city of Versailles, which we had to skip during our previous trip to Paris in February 2022 for Firuza's birthday celebration.

We began visualizing a wonderful vacation, these were our 25A. Deep inside I felt that everything would work out, because my soul really wanted this trip.

The most difficult part was that in the very beginning, we couldn't find concert tickets, everything was sold out. At some point a few dates became available, but the seats weren't situated together. So we didn't buy the tickets, we were waiting for a sign from the Universe. You can only proceed to take action after the Universe delivers its 50, remember?

We thought "well, if there aren't any signs, then it's not our path again." As we surrendered, all of a sudden, one of the concert dates became available, there were only two tickets available and they were right next to each other. We immediately bought them. That was it, the Universe showed us the best way and we followed it, we carried out the second part of our task, the 25B. We first set an intention

(25A), then we received a confirmation (the 50) and only after that we acted. We booked a hotel, bought airplane and concert tickets. That was our 25B. Everything was exactly according to the formula, which is why it turned out to be effortless and simple.

Startup

Using the formula 25A+50+25B, we created and launched our startup Floovly (www.floovly.com). Our mission is to support women on their self-development and self-love journey by raising the level of awareness and improving their overall wellbeing through meditation, breathwork techniques, yoga etc.

In 2019, we came up with the idea of a global project, but nothing was working out because we weren't doing it according to the formula, we didn't know it back then. Once we started applying the formula 25A+50+25B (still without knowing the formula, but intuitively taking the right steps), we received an invitation to move to Europe and start our project there. We set an intention, our 25A. We kept our project in mind, created a development plan, made the calculations. Then we waited. We let go of the situation and waited until the Universe responded.

As soon as the Universe delivered its 50, as soon as we received an invitation to launch our project in Europe, we completed our second part, the 25B. That was the actual relocation and the launch of our startup.

Initially, the idea behind Floovly was a marketplace for delivering flowers in Europe, then we transitioned to a weekly flower subscription service with a focus on wellbeing and mental health. And only in 2022 we had an epiphany. We realized what we're meant to do - launch a global project that is going to help millions of women around the world to become more conscious, to believe in themselves and create a fulfilling life. On our platform women from all over the world receive self-growth tools from the best coaches and mentors in their niches.

There are no coincidences in life

Meeting Firuza was not a coincidence. We were destined to be together, our souls agreed to meet here on Earth in order to go through this path of growth and mindfulness together.

We attended the same high school, I knew her classmates and she knew mine. But surprisingly we didn't get to know each other during our high school years. After high school we both moved to different countries.

Many years later in 2015, when we both returned to Baku, I was invited for an interview to the company where Firuza was working at the time. But we didn't meet there either as I wasn't satisfied with the offered position and didn't agree with the conditions.

We met a little later, in another company, that was in 2017. Firuza had just started working there and I was about to quit. We managed to exchange contacts and soon started dating. But not right away. For about 2 months I couldn't convince her to go on a date with me, she kept rejecting me and made it clear that we were different. Do you think I listened to her?

We now realize that our meeting could have happened much earlier if we were conscious enough. We both dreamed of a certain type of relationship, an equal one, where everything is done together. The idea of getting married and having kids because you have to or because you're getting older (how old is too old?) didn't sit well with us. We craved genuine, true love.

We set our intentions, our 25A. The Universe kept drawing us together until both of us realized that we found our partner. These were the signs of the Universe, her 50. Our actions, 25B - we started dating, launched a business together, got married, relocated, and now live in love and harmony.

Quantum physics

If you don't believe that you are capable of creating your desired life, start exploring quantum physics. Yes, you heard that right. Quantum physics says that nothing can appear in our reality until we draw our attention to it.

That is, you have to imagine something, pay attention to it and only then you will see it appear in your reality. Nothing happens without our attention. Our attention determines the reality. This means that we need to focus our attention on the things we desire to attract into our lives. If you want wealth, you can have it! Just stop thinking about being broke and the lack of money. Think, visualize and feel wealthy. Visualize what it feels like to live in luxury and comfort.

Circumstances and events are all consequences of our thoughts. Then how come we ourselves attract negative events into our life? Yes, both positive and negative. Our energy, our consciousness, our mind can shape anything. There is even a name for it - the Observer Effect.

Thoughts and feelings can influence and affect every area of our life, all aspects of it. This confirms what I said earlier. We can create our own reality with the power of our thoughts and feelings. We are powerful and we can change any circumstances and reach any heights, conquer any peaks. This is the 25A, where we set our intentions and visualize, using our thoughts and feelings.

The quantum field (which is everything around us and we ourselves are in the quantum field) does not react to our desires. It reacts to our emotional state of being. When I told you about 25A, I mentioned that it is crucial to be able to emotionally feel the things we want to manifest in our life.

In the process of shaping your intentions, consider and observe the alignment of your thoughts and feelings. There are many different realities out there, but we are able choose the one that feels right for us. To achieve this, we need to become a vibrational match to our new desired reality. This implies that if we want to find love, we must radiate love, rather than complaining that we are not loved. It's all about the vibrations that we radiate and based on that we receive what we send out into the world.

If we crave affection in relationships but we radiate negativity, we will find ourselves in a reality where we aren't happy. To be in harmonious relationships with others, we ourselves must radiate the energy of love, achieve inner harmony and shine positivity into the world.

When our vibration aligns with the vibration of the reality that we desire, we will be pulled into this reality. It is essential to keep in mind the vision of the life that we desire and to amplify it with emotions and feelings that we will experience in that desired future.

In the next chapter, we will talk about limiting beliefs that block us from fully using this formula.

Beliefs and Fears

Stories that clearly reflect my belief system

Beliefs are programs that are imprinted into our subconscious mind and these programs determine how we live our lives.

There can be negative (limiting) and positive beliefs. They've been embedded into our subconscious mind since childhood or even before our birth, and control our life until we decide to replace them.

So what about our beliefs?

They are actually limiting us from tapping into the full potential of the formula 25A + 50 + 25B.

Once we have less limiting beliefs we'll be better at noticing the signs of the Universe, understanding them and taking corresponding action.

There was one specific insecurity that bothered me. When we started dating with Firuza, we used to dream about building our own home, the place where we would live, the kind of work we'd do, how we'd enjoy life, travel etc. I used to dream, just like Firuza, of a luxurious and comfortable lifestyle, but after a while, my insecurities began to surface. I started saying and believing that I actually don't need all those material things, a luxury villa, an extravagant yacht, a private jet, an expensive car, designer clothes and so on. It turns out, I was simply scared that I would have to work extremely hard in order to have it all. I had no idea how I'd achieve it, without money, connections, and actually I thought, I wasn't that smart.

These limiting beliefs (that shape our actions, thoughts and words) were preventing me from trying on a luxurious and comfortable lifestyle. How did I eventually understand that these are all limiting beliefs?

I made a list of things that I enjoy and things that bring me fulfilment. This list included the sea, sun, sky, sand, tranquillity, peace. As I made the list I thought to myself: "Since I enjoy all of those things, I don't really need to give up on my dreams."

After all, I love the sun, the water, the sky, the clouds. I really appreciate peace, comfort, I value my time. This means that a luxury lifestyle suits me very well – my own mansion with a private beach, my own island, my own yacht, where I'd relax with my family and where no one would bother us. Having a private jet is important too as I love to travel and I don't want to waste time at airports, arriving three hours in advance, being checked by different control services and jostling with the crowds. By human design, I am a manifestor, peace and comfort are extremely important to me. And this is what my soul is attracted to.

So, I had to fight with my belief system in order to convince myself that I truly needed all the things that I dreamt of.

Previously in life, when I aimed for a higher salary, I didn't really want it. How did I come to this realization? Very simple. If I really wanted a higher salary, I'd be happier when I was offered it. But this never happened.

My salary increased, yet I couldn't find anything that would really bring me joy. I would always look for ways to spend my savings. In addition, I tried to free myself of the responsibility for my own life - I didn't try to create anything myself, I simply wanted to invest money somewhere and get rich overnight. I didn't know what to do because I didn't know what I truly wanted. And I didn't know what I truly wanted, because I didn't listen to the voice of my soul.

It's interesting how we, humans, are very similar. When we don't know what to do, we end up doing things that make us feel even worse. When you don't know what to do, it's time to start listening to the voice of your soul. It is whispering the truth but never shouting.

The belief that success can only be achieved through hard work, through blood, sweat and tears, has played a huge role in my life.

For instance, I genuinely believed that you can't achieve anything without facing difficulties and hence, I always found myself in situations where everything was extremely difficult.

There was a time when I earned money by distributing brochures on the streets of Moscow, while it was -35 degrees Celsius. I truly believed that I had to endure these difficult times. But I created these difficulties myself.

Of course, it was possible to find an easier job. I could find a company that would hire me remotely, for example, and I'd work from the comfort of my warm dorm room. But seems like it was easier for me to do it the hard way rather than finding an easier solution.

If I knew the principles of the formula 25A + 50 + 25B, I would have certainly always followed the path of least resistance, without needing to sacrifice my health and nervous system.

My belief that "difficult is normal" led to me eating stale bread and drinking tap water because I didn't have enough money. Can you imagine what our own belief system does to us? If I knew the formula back then, I wouldn't have clung to the belief that life is difficult. And even more so, I wouldn't have nourished this belief with emotions and feelings, which ended up amplifying it even more. I would have noticed other possibilities and easier paths. I wouldn't have tried to break into doors that aren't mine. I would have only chosen my door.

But these beliefs, deeply rooted in our subconscious mind, determine the outcome of our lives. That's why it's so important to reprogram our limiting beliefs that hold us back and replace them with positive ones.

Have you ever been hit by a huge bus?

Well, I was. Around the age of 9–10 I was hit by a huge bus. As the bus hit me (in Azerbaijan these buses were called "alabash"), I bounced off, made a flip and fell face down on the pavement. People gathered around me and I heard someone say that an urgent surgery was required. I got so scared that I jumped right up and continued my way as if nothing had happened. My face was one huge bruise. But I was safe and sound.

One other time, I was about 12 year old, a car drove over my feet. My toes hurt for a little while, that's all.

At the age of 14 a nail went through my foot, not very deep. I immediately reacted and pulled it out.

One more time, around the same age, I almost fell into a deep pit: I leaned on the bricks to see what was down there, there was emptiness, a foundation for a new building was being constructed. I suddenly began to slide down but miraculously I managed to jump back.

While living in Moscow, I was hit by a car once again, but nothing serious happened. I was ready for the hit and covered myself with my gym bag.

In India, in Goa, at the age of 25, I swam in the raging ocean and found myself in a mini pool surrounded by rocks where I couldn't get out. On one side very slippery rocks wouldn't allow me to climb over them, on the other, endless waves wouldn't let me swim out of this mini pool. The waves kept hitting me and the rocks. I had to make a decision fast as I was being thrown from one rock to another by the waves. Miraculously, I got out of this situation too.

During the same time in Goa, I got attacked by a pack of dogs. It happened during the night, more than ten dogs started barking and chasing me. I fell to the ground, horrified but as soon as their growling snouts were on top of my face, I jumped up abruptly and started screaming back at them. Luckily, the neighbours came to rescue me and even applied some healing cream on my elbows as I injured them when I fell down.

After each of these events, I felt invincible and powerful. I must confess, I liked this feeling.

Each time, my subconscious mind created these events, these difficult situations, confirming my beliefs. I created all these challenges so that after overcoming them I could feel invincible. The subconscious mind always tries to affirm your beliefs and finds evidence in the outside world.

When I was in high school, 9th or 10th grade, three guys, much older than me, beat me up in the school yard. I was covered in blood, my nose was broken. I strongly felt the injustice of the world around me. When I was called for questioning, the police treated me as if I was the one who beat up those three guys. The investigator told me, "We're in Azerbaijan, here we can reverse the situation against you and your family." That immediately brought back memories of the time when my family was attacked and our house, our belongings were taken away from us (the story I shared in the very beginning of the book). That feeling of helplessness and fear resurfaced once again. The belief was "this place is not safe and anyone can hurt me." I felt like I was incapable of changing my circumstances, at least in that country and so I decided to leave.

That was the strongest motivation to leave Azerbaijan. Since I found myself in such challenging circumstances, it seems to me that there must have been signs along the way, signs that were guiding me. But when you neglect the signs, when you ignore them, you end up in unpleasant situations which force you to finally take action.

I moved to Moscow with a luggage of bitter experiences. As years went by I was able to recover, only on the outside though.

I picked up another belief – I can do everything better on my own. While living in Moscow, I was prescribed some medications, I had to take injections, but I didn't know anyone who could do this for me. Visiting the clinic every time and waiting in line wasn't an option, as I had to attend classes and work.

I decided to do the injections myself. I was warned that I could insert the needle incorrectly, hurt myself seriously and it could even result in numbness, but this didn't stop me. I asked a friend that studied medicine to help me with the instructions via Skype. I bought rubbing alcohol, cotton pads, syringes, and the medicine itself; and every day I did the injections myself. It was extremely uncomfortable and I'd have cramps which made it difficult to insert or pull out the needle properly. Once while giving myself the injection, as I couldn't stretch back enough, the needle slipped out and I had to insert the needle twice.

These stories clearly demonstrate that our belief system prevents us from thinking differently. Our beliefs paralyze us, forcing us to act in certain ways and not otherwise. We begin to follow a certain pattern of behavior and become very predictable and hence, vulnerable.

After nine years in Moscow, I wanted to return to Baku. I naively believed that since I was no longer the same person, everything back home had changed as well.

That wasn't the case. I found myself in another situation that may seem very unfair to you, but it all happened because of my inner belief that life was unfair to me. This belief had been planted in my mind many years ago and this situation just confirmed what I believed to be true.

The CEO of the company where I worked as an analyst sent his security guards to beat me and demand back the money they had previously spent on my job-related training (priced at 1500 US dollars). Can you guess why? Because when I decided to quit it had only been a month since the training. After returning from the training, I was invited to work for another company with much better terms. I was delighted and couldn't even suspect that the CEO would not want to let me go.

In civilized organizations there should be appropriate agreements in place for similar cases, as to avoid any misunderstandings and assaults. After all, I wasn't an important employee, they didn't even want to raise my salary, although initially that was promised numerous times. I made my conclusions - I'm not needed here, I'm not valuable, and no one will be upset if I leave.

But the CEO decided to demonstrate his strength and power. To some of you, this will seem like a terrible story, very unfair, but for some, it might be common (I hope there are very few of you). The bottom line is that I attracted this situation because I sincerely believed that the world is unfair to me, and that I don't live in a safe place. The world will not try to prove you wrong, it will reflect exactly what you think of it.

In my previous workplaces in Moscow, if an employee was sent for job-related training, there were always contracts that indicated when you had the right to quit the job or if you left earlier, you'd have to pay for the training if that was originally communicated to the employee. No one beat or threatened you. In my case, there were no such contracts. Moreover, instead of the 1 500 US dollars, they wanted me to pay 5 000 US dollars. You must admit, my belief about injustice worked in all its glory. I was being charged an amount more than the amount that was paid for my training – a typical example of how our own beliefs become our reality. There is another lesson here. You need to be decisive and act immediately when you feel that the time has come. Don't be afraid, don't hesitate. Because fear and hesitation often lead to terrible consequences, just like in my case. I wanted to leave much earlier but my fear of uncertainty took over.

The financial director forged the documents, and drew up a fake contract, which mentioned this new amount. I was astonished because I knew the precise amount as I was the one who submitted the payment for the training. But they chose to show me their strength and power by humiliating me. I'm leaving it to their conscience. It's obvious that their souls had lost their way. Through this example we can clearly see how my belief "people can shamelessly mock me and walk all over me" was reflected in my reality.

The head of security and his right hand beat me, and threatened me and my family if I ever tell anyone about this situation or if I don't return the money.

Injustice again? History repeats itself, have you noticed? Here are the exact words the head of security told me: "Our boss is very powerful and he can do whatever he wants."

I heard literally the same words from the investigator 12 years ago when I was beaten up in the schoolyard by three older guys. Now, are you convinced that our beliefs shape our reality?

My mind reproduced my beliefs into the physical reality. The beliefs that others can humiliate me, beat me, rob me.

Neural pathways

Neurons are brain cells that play a key role in our functioning. Neurons form neural pathways.

We create new neural pathways when we engage in a new activity, that's unfamiliar to our brain and our perception.

You can create new neural pathways by starting a new business, getting a new job, or doing something unfamiliar, something new. For example, you can start painting, singing, or playing a musical instrument if you haven't done that before.

New neural pathways are formed even as you begin to think differently. If you used to think that wealth is bad, it's unsafe and it belongs to a select few, by replacing these thoughts with "wealth is safe, it is easy to become wealthy" you can start changing your reality.

You create new neural pathways even when you return home using a different route or take a stroll in a new place. That's why travel affects us in such a positive way: new people, new culture, food, lifestyle, absolutely everything is new.

You can not only create neural pathways but also strengthen them. By creating and strengthening your neural pathways, you think broader, make faster decisions and have more trust in yourself. The more neural pathways, the better our brain functions, and this in turn leads to improvements in our life. This has been backed by science. We strengthen our neural pathways with repetition.

Dutch train effect

While we were traveling by train from the Netherlands to Belgium, Firuza urgently wanted to use the restroom. Armed with anti-bacterial towels, she began her bathroom search. She noticed a crowd in front of one of the restrooms and assumed they were all waiting in line. As it turns out, they were not waiting in line, although it was obvious they wouldn't mind using the bathroom themselves. Except they assumed it was dirty and smelled unpleasant, and hence they didn't even dare to open the bathroom door.

Remember, this was just their assumption.

A dilemma arises: to listen to these people who warned her not to open the bathroom door and wait for another two hours or open the door and check how bad it is. Firuza chose the latter and guess what? It was clean.

This makes you wonder. Not a single person wanted to check for himself. Based only on their assumptions, they were afraid to open the door.

Besides, they dared to take responsibility and convince Firuza that it was better not to go in there.

Can you see what type of limitations people have? I'm curious to ask these people, "where is your audacity when it comes to your own life? When you need to take responsibility and start changing your life: starting a new job, launching a business, getting into new relationships, saying no when you don't feel like it?." When it comes to starting your own business, for example, you find millions of excuses why not to, simply based on your assumptions and beliefs- it's risky, and there are no guarantees. There is only one guarantee in life - we will all die.

It's fascinating that these beliefs are formed not even as a result of their own experiences. In addition to that, these types of people try to bring others down so that they too continue living an unhappy life.

What would have happened if Firuza listened to them? We always have a choice: freeze and endure or move forward and win.

Fears and Commands

We live in a world where we are constantly afraid of something or someone. Have you thought about the fact that when we were little, we were not afraid of anything - we could approach large dogs and hit them in the muzzle, and we were not afraid to slip and fall?

How we learn to walk deserves special attention, I really love this example. We constantly fall until we learn to walk and we never say: "this isn't working out, I tried to walk ten times already, I'm going to quit."

We keep trying to walk until we walk. There is no other way. We don't need motivation, we don't complain, and we don't say that it's difficult, impossible, and beyond our power. No, we never say that. All children achieve this goal, and we all end up walking. So why is it that later in life we are afraid of failure? How did we even come up with the idea that something might not work out?

Where do these fears come from? These are programs that were installed in our subconscious mind by society, our family, acquaintances, the system, and religion. Since childhood, they warn us, rather than explaining. We are told what to do and what not to do based on previous experiences. This is clearly wrong, but that's life, that's how it is. That's how we were all raised. Some parents awaken, become mindful, and bring up their children differently, explaining why and how rather than forbidding. Since our childhood, we keep hearing "it's impossible to go there", "don't do it, it's wrong", "you're old enough", "it's not the way to do it", "you're not a girl, why are you crying" or "you're not a boy, play with dolls, why do you play with cars" and so on. All these beliefs, and programs are recorded and rooted in our subconscious mind and we end up being helpless. We end up being insecure and afraid to make a move.

There is an effective way to overcome your fear.

A command is nothing more than an instruction that is given to our body and mind that helps us overcome our fears and change our belief system.

Using this technique Firuza was able to get rid of her fear of dogs. Previously, dogs would always approach us and we'd have to hide away. This really annoyed us and we decided to put an end to this fear once and for all.

Firuza gave herself a command: I am comfortable around dogs. Every time there was a dog near her, she'd look at the dog and repeat to herself "I am comfortable around you."

After a couple of days, we started witnessing miracles. Dogs not only didn't approach us anymore, but they also started running away from us, in the most literal sense of the word. And her fear and anxiety were completely gone.

These types of commands can also help us get rid of any addictions. For instance, I was able to overcome my incredibly strong craving for sweets. I just gave myself the command "Thank you, but I'm fine without sweets." It's as if I found the switch and turned it off.

You can also get rid of discomfort using positive commands. Firuza had some pain in her body, so what she did was, she simply told her body that everything was fine, that there was nothing to worry about, and that she felt comfortable and healthy. Guess what happened next? The body, as if having heard the message, realized that there was no need to be scared, to worry or defend itself, and obeyed like a child. The pain was gone.

We can give commands to our body and mind to feel better or get rid of unhealthy habits. We can show our body that we're fine, that there is no need to turn on the defense mechanism and cause pain and anxiety. If you can have a heart-to-heart conversation with your body, it will listen. In order for the commands technique to work for you, you need to increase the level of your energy and awareness. You can do this with the help of exercises that are further given in this book.

If you need to solve a specific issue, let's not call it a problem, you can easily find a quick solution by using "commands".

Instead of puzzling over a possible solution and trying to carry out actions, that in your opinion seem logical, you have a chance to come up with a quick solution and most importantly, achieve it with ease. All you need is to be mindful and give a specific command to your subconscious mind and body.

Let me show you an example. If you urgently need to decide what to wear, but you can't seem to make a fast decision, you need to stop, close your eyes, calm down, and ask yourself the question: what should I wear if I want to feel comfortable?

If you want to stand out, ask yourself: "what should I wear to look and feel stunning today?" Listen to yourself, the answer will come. This is you asking your soul, it knows exactly what's best for you.

Our subconscious mind is not always aware of what's optimal, and most suitable for us, it tries to lead based on past experience, but this is not always right for us. The subconscious doesn't take into account the desires of the soul and proclaims itself as the main decision-maker. Our goal is to create harmony between the soul, body, and mind. This way decisions are made with ease.

Many of us don't even suspect how powerful we are. We are unaware of our ability to convince our subconscious mind of anything we desire. We always have a choice - we can live with the old programs, limiting beliefs, and unnecessary judgements or free ourselves and let our souls enjoy this wonderful ride, the journey of becoming conscious and responsible for our own lives.

Don't be afraid to desire, to dream and set goals, even if you don't have the resources right now. You can't wait until you have the money to set goals. The world functions in a completely different way. First set goals - 25A, then wait for the signs from the Universe, the 50, which could be new connections, people, a certain amount of money, or anything else. After that, effortlessly carry out the remaining 25B, and take action.

If you find it hard to believe that you have the money to accomplish your goals, when, in fact, you don't have any, here's some advice.

Consider that your money is in a safety box, the keys to which are held by the Universe. The Universe decides when and how much money to give you. It sends you as much as you need for your purposes. You don't need to see the entire amount of money. When you have a goal that is aligned with your soul, the Universe will hand you the required amount, it will transfer it to your bank account or find another way to reach you.

The following chapter provides exercises that will help increase your level of energy and awareness, which are both necessary to successfully implement the formula.

Exercises

I did not invent these exercises, they exist in various forms and below I am sharing with you my modified version of these exercises and techniques.

These exercises will help you raise your awareness level, get rid of any limiting beliefs, and hence, allow you to apply the formula with ease. It is crucial to shift your mindset and learn to feel yourself, your soul, and your body and to learn to talk to yourself.

The more aware you are, the higher your energy level and vibrations are. This is important to get the best results after completing the exercises.

We also share various exercises and techniques in Floovly Club, where we organize workshops aimed at increasing awareness and raising vibrations. We invite experts and coaches to lead mindset workshops, breathwork sessions, yoga, meditations, hypnotherapy, and much more.

Breathing exercises

Close your eyes, and straighten your back. Slowly take a deep breath through the nose and exhale through the mouth. Concentrate on your breath, and send away your thoughts.

As thoughts appear, catch the thought and return your attention to breathing.

This technique is very simple, but nevertheless incredibly effective. It helps you increase your level of consciousness, which is required to use the possibilities of the 25A + 50 + 25B formula to its fullest potential. It is when you focus on breathing that you are in the present moment.

Keep breathing this way for 5-10 minutes, you can keep going on for longer if you wish.

You will soon begin to notice how your overall well-being is improving.

Over time, you will become more attentive to yourself and the world around you, you will become more conscious.

Meditation

Practice mindfulness through meditation.

It is the most powerful tool that helps you become more conscious and more open to receiving information, as well as being able to feel your body, and your emotions and follow the path of your thoughts. This in turn leads to the ability to visualize and feel your desired reality with ease and flow.

Find a quiet and peaceful place, sit down and close your eyes. Focus on your breathing or your body. Feel your body.

Track the sensations in your body. Try not to move, not to think about anything. Sit this way for 5-10 minutes.

Meditation will help you calm down and organize your thoughts.

Affirmations

These are short positive phrases, that can influence your subconscious mind and have the power to reprogram it.

In other words, affirmations are positive statements that help change our limiting beliefs.

Everyone has limiting beliefs. It's essential to timely recognize their existence, identify them and start replacing them with positive ones, this can be done through affirmations.

It's crucial to determine what kind of limiting beliefs you have. Start by observing yourself and tracking your thoughts, feelings, words, and actions relative to specific circumstances, situations, and people. Catch yourself every time you make a statement about a certain subject.

The first step is to recognize that everyone has limiting beliefs. Don't feel guilty.

The second step is to become more attentive to ourselves, and the things we say and feel. At this stage, you need to identify and catch your limiting beliefs.

Step three. This is when we work with these limiting beliefs and replace them with positive affirmations, repeating specific statements and feeling the emotions that arise with these statements. Affirmations will reprogram your subconscious mind only if they are reinforced with emotions. You should feel what you are stating in your body. You can create these affirmations for yourself, depending on your specific limiting beliefs.

You can speak the affirmations out loud or repeat them mentally to yourself. Focus on the feelings that you experience. Enjoy the emotions that are born with the affirmations, so that your body believes you and gives a signal to your mind to start overwriting the old beliefs with the new ones. This is how you reprogram your subconscious mind and get rid of the limiting beliefs that prevent you from living a mindful and happy life.

You can also take a piece of paper and note all your thoughts about life, money, relationships, people, and so on. Anything that comes to mind. Usually limiting beliefs begin with the words: I know that or I am sure that.

For example, I am sure that all rich people are bad. Why? Because they steal money from the common people or because they buy expensive things when there is so much poverty in the world. "The rich are bad" - that's the belief that prevents many people from living a fulfilling life.

Do you know why you aren't wealthy? Because you have such a belief. If I am a good person but I'm broke then the rich who are not broke must be bad. There is a confrontation between you and them. Such limiting beliefs won't get you far.

If you realize that you might have a similar belief, here's an affirmation that will help you:

I choose to be wealthy and kind.

Another popular saying goes like this: "A lot of money means a lot of problems."

Do you see what's happening here? Your subconscious mind finds excuses not to start a business. Because that would mean that you need to leave your comfort zone, and for the subconscious mind this is a very unpleasant process. It loves what's familiar, which are the old programs and beliefs.

The subconscious mind will do anything to protect you from taking new actions. It doesn't want you to become wealthy, why should it? It's been fine all this time. The subconscious mind will use the old programs and beliefs to influence your decisions in every possible way. Thus, for instance, it will stop you from starting your own business. It will justify this by claiming that it's too risky, "Why do you need a different life, we are doing fine."

If you want to create a better life for yourself you need to trick your mind, to outsmart it. How can you be content knowing that one body part is ruling your life and setting the limits?

The subconscious mind loves its comfort zone - everything that's familiar, and it will fight to keep everything as it is - the same work, the same relationships, the same life, etc. For the subconscious mind "familiar" means safe. It doesn't care that you hate your job or that you're unhappy in this relationship or that you are bored with your life. Don't expect your subconscious mind to support you on this quest.

When beliefs such as "rich people are bad" or "rich people are unhappy" are stored in your subconscious, the mind benefits from them, it uses these beliefs to manipulate you. "You don't want to be unhappy, so you shouldn't want to be wealthy", the subconscious suggests.

Try this affirmation to turn your limiting belief into a positive one:

It's safe for me to be wealthy.

Remember to attach emotions and feelings when repeating this affirmation several times a day, for 21 days. In fact, you can create affirmations for yourself relating to any type of occasions and beliefs.

If you have a limiting belief "the more money you have, the more problems you face" then the subconscious mind will justify this belief to you, "We don't need problems, let's leave the situation as it is and live like everyone else, a normal life."

In reality, there is no real danger. On the contrary, the real danger is living a life that doesn't bring us joy, being in relationships that don't serve us, working at a job we hate, or doing something we don't enjoy. s

That's the real risk for me - to live life doing something I don't like, to live where I don't want to and with people, I don't enjoy spending time with. We deserve everything we can imagine. Keep this in mind next time you let this little part of your body manipulate you.

Visualization

What should you visualize? Absolutely anything that you desire to have in your life. Set aside 10-15 minutes a day for visualization purposes and practice it several times a day. Most importantly, visualize the most vivid details and keep in mind that when you're visualizing you need to place yourself as the main character, not an observer. Here's a way to feel like you're present in this visualization: imagine looking at your own hands and feet at the beginning of the visualization practice. Start visualizing everything that you desire. Visualize your dream life: what's it like, who are you in this life, what do you do, where do you live, whom do you live with, who surrounds you, who is your family, what are they like, what's your relationship with them.

The best time to visualize is the moment after you wake up or right before falling asleep. Those are special periods of time between wakefulness and sleep called the theta state. In this state, the power of your visualization gets amplified.

For instance, visualize yourself in your dream home, surrounded by loved ones, being served delicious food. Imagine yourself laughing, and talking. Strengthen the visualization with your senses. Let all the senses participate - hearing, sight, smell, taste, and touch. Let your ears, eyes, nose, tongue, and skin help you create a dream life through the process of visualization.

Feel the emotions, how you see, smell, what you think, how you look. The more detailed and vivid you can visualize yourself in your new life, the sooner you will attain it.

It is crucial not only to visualize and imagine your dream life in all its glory but to feel the emotions of what you're visualizing. Feeling these emotions might seem a little difficult. However, with daily practice, you'll learn to feel and experience emotions with your entire body.

Visualize yourself becoming successful, wealthy, and happy, and experience these emotions, feel this joy in your body. Visualize down to the smallest detail.

Healing Technique

Did you know that you could send a beam of golden light to parts of your body that are in pain and this would heal them? We use this technique whenever Firuza and I experience any kind of pain, from toothache to pain in the back, muscles, and joints. We concentrate on the part of the body that needs healing and direct a beam of golden light there. Imagine how this beam of light descends from the sky and enters your body.

Remember, that our body is a self-healing system, and we have the power to heal ourselves without medical intervention.

For this technique to be effective, you have to pay attention (remember quantum physics) to the area that is causing discomfort and direct a golden stream of light to that specific part of your body.

Try it even if you don't believe me. Then send me a message and tell me how surprised you are to find out that you can actually heal yourself without any outside help or intervention.

Simply close your eyes, direct a stream of light coming from above into that area, and hold for a few seconds or minutes. And witness for yourself how effective this method is. It is also the most natural way of healing.

Gratitude

We've made it a habit to thank the Universe for everything we have.

That could be something big and expensive as well as something small like a delicious breakfast.

Keep a gratitude journal and thank the Universe for everything you have and for everything you desire to attract into your life.

Express gratitude in the present tense even if your intention hasn't been achieved yet. You can say, "I am grateful for my new car." Don't say, "I am grateful for the new car that I will buy."

You can feel gratitude for absolutely anything. It upsets us when people say that there is nothing to be grateful for.

Don't they understand that even if things don't go according to their plan, they can still be grateful for simply being alive? They are given the opportunity to live, create and enjoy life. Be grateful for your loved ones, your family, for everyone dear to you, and for the fact that they are healthy and alive.

Be grateful for the peaceful sky above your head, for the beautiful clouds, for the wonderful sun, for the fresh and clean air, for the warm and golden sand, for the clean water, for our Earth.

Raise your vibrations

If you want to raise your vibrations and energy, try doing more of the things you enjoy. This in turn will create new neural pathways in the brain and you will soon begin to notice changes in your life.

Here's what we do for the contentment of our soul: we read every day, often play chess, and paint on weekends. We also play tennis, go on beach walks, and swim in the ocean. All these activities recharge us and give us the energy and strength to create the life we dream of.

Spend time engaging in any type of activity that brings you happiness and joy. This will leave you feeling energized and inspired.

This energy will allow you to hear your soul's desires and take action based on what you truly want. By raising your vibration, you will also get better at hearing your body.

Firuza and I have achieved incredible results precisely thanks to increasing our awareness and raising our vibrations. We switched to a healthier diet. We could still eat something that's not considered healthy if we feel like it. But generally, we eat what our body needs and asks for. Headaches and fatigue are gone, for instance. We feel supercharged.

We began eating intuitively. We realized that we feel so much better now. This way we give our body more time to recharge and rest. We also try to drink lots of water.

Silence

Here's something new that you could also try out. This exercise may seem strange to you, but it will help you raise your level of awareness.

On Sundays, from the moment we wake up at around 6-7 am until noon, we don't talk to each other, and don't use our phones or any other gadgets. During this silent time, we slow down and become more conscious. Our thoughts become more organized, we are calmer and as a result, we feel more high-spirited.

You can spend this time painting, playing chess, reading books, and jotting down your plans, or to-do lists. You can use pen and paper, but not electronic devices with screens. And communication with others isn't allowed.

This exercise helps you pay closer attention to yourself, your emotions, feelings, words, actions, and reactions to events, situations, and people.

Observe yourself, your reaction to the outside world, and what you feel and think throughout your experiences.

Slowly, you will start noticing interesting things about yourself, things you hadn't realized before.

Give what you want to receive

If you're seeking love, give love first. If you feel lack of money, share a portion of your money with someone, and make a donation. For several years now, Firuza and I have been allocating a percentage of our income as donations to various organizations and people. Sometimes we help out a stranger on the street and sometimes we approach orphanages.

By sending money into the world, and money is energy, we create a better world for everyone. We love money and money loves us. For instance, by donating money, we were able to help heal a few people whose conditions were uncurable.

Don't be ashamed of money, instead desire it, but focus on the things you need the money for. It could be buying a house or something smaller like a new phone.

It's important to visualize and feel the emotions of what you desire, the things that money will help you achieve. Thus, attracting these things into your life.

Often people tell us that they don't have any extra money for donations.

Even when we had only one hundred dollars, we still tried to help. You can donate one dollar or one, five, or ten percent of your earnings. I'm sure you can do it. You'd be surprised but miracles will follow in the form of new opportunities, sources of income, etc.

Abundance energy will flow into your life. Everything will unfold in your favor. All events and situations will develop in the best possible way. People will even call you lucky.

Kindness and doing good are inherent in us. We humans are not just a body. We are body, mind, and soul. We are multidimensional, highly spiritual beings. And it's in our nature to love and to spread love.

We are all united. We are one. But, at the same time, we are separated from each other into bodies, so that each one of us can have his own experience on Earth. As souls, it's alien to us to cause damage and harm. But, inside the body, we get to feel negative emotions and express them. Souls tend to express joy and love. Inside the body, we forget about our true source. To remember who we truly are, we need to raise our awareness.

If at some point you feel like you're missing a certain thing and you feel hopeless and unsure what to do next, the best thing you can do is share that thing you're lacking with others. For example, if you feel lack of warmth and love, start taking care of others and you'll notice how your circumstances begin to shift.

Especially during the times when you experience this feeling of lack, you should be more eager to support and take care of others. Don't have enough money? Find someone who has the same problem (lack of money) and do something kind for that person, buy something, or donate money. What will happen next? You're probably thinking, "well, what could possibly happen, I'll give away all my money and won't be able to save for my next dream "toy", right?"

What if I tell you that as soon as you share what you have, you'll receive more money and everything you need to realize your dream?

Future Self

Here's a very effective exercise that will help you create the best version of yourself. You will have to go through a few questions in order to design this image of the ideal future version of you. This exercise is connected to the subconscious mind.

Question 1: What does the future version of you enjoy?

What do you enjoy doing? Answer honestly, what would you do if you had unlimited time, energy, money, and other resources? What would you dedicate your time to? What would you be doing? Maybe you dream of painting, or being an author, maybe you love to travel and discover new places. What gives you pleasure: singing birds, sunsets, sunrises, being alone with yourself, surrounding yourself with loved ones, being in nature, delicious food. Write down everything that comes to mind.

_____

_____

_____
_____
_____
_____
_____
_____

Question 2: What does your future version look like?

What does the future you look like? This pertains to your appearance, or rather, the appearance of the future version of yourself. This is the perfect version of you. Try to describe yourself in as much detail as possible: what type of clothes you're wearing, the colors, the textures, how the clothes make you feel, what's your hairstyle like, what's your body like, what's your scent. Describe everything that pertains to your appearance.

_____
_____
_____
_____

_____
_____
_____
_____
_____

Question 3: What the future version of you does with his/her time?

How and where do you spend your time? Who do you spend most of your time with? What's your future self doing throughout the day? Do you spend your time in front of your laptop, or your phone, do you play online games, or spend time on social networks or do you read, play sports, walk, or spend time with your family, relatives, and friends? Do you spend time doing what you love or do you spend most of your time working? Do you have time for the things your soul desires to experience?

_____
_____
_____
_____
_____

_____
_____
_____
_____

Question 4: How does your future version think?

What do you think about? Imagine the ideal future version of you and imagine, what would this person think about. How would you think in specific situations? Would you get angry, or desperate or would you have absolute faith that everything happens for the best? Would you view each event, situation, or circumstance as an opportunity or would you panic when something doesn't go as planned?

_____
_____
_____
_____
_____
_____
_____
_____

Question 5: How does your future self behave?

How do you behave in various situations? Are you generous, calm, and confident? Do you have faith that everything turns out to be fine, do you act authentically, do you motivate others around you?

_____
_____
_____
_____
_____
_____
_____
_____
_____
_____

Question 6: How does your future self feel?

What does this ideal version of you feel? Does he/she feel restless or peaceful, fearful or joyful? Are you anxious or in harmony with yourself? Do you feel that the Universe loves and supports you? Describe in detail the feelings of your future self.

_____
_____
_____
_____
_____
_____
_____
_____
_____

Question 7: How does the future version of you feel about himself/herself?

What do you think of yourself? How do you take care of yourself? What do you do for your soul, your body, and mind? Do you play any sports, or go to the spa? Do you read books, do you travel?

How do you feel about yourself when you make mistakes? Are you kind to yourself? Do you treat yourself with understanding and love, even when you make mistakes? Or do you blame yourself?

Be gentle with yourself. Treat yourself with understanding, love, and compassion. Your attitude towards yourself will be conveyed to others, they will feel your gentle and compassionate attitude towards yourself and they, in turn, will treat you with understanding and care as well. Give yourself permission to make mistakes, forgive and love yourself unconditionally.

_____
_____
_____
_____
_____
_____
_____
_____
_____

Question 8: How does your future self treat others?

Imagine how the ideal version of you relates to others, what does he/she do for others, and what does he/she think of people? How does he/she behave towards them? Do you treat people with respect and love?

_____
_____
_____
_____
_____
_____
_____
_____
_____

Question 9: What does the future version of you eat?

What do you eat on a daily basis? Is it healthy food? How many times a day do you eat, do you like to eat fruit and vegetables? Is your food delicious? Do you eat what you want to eat? Do you eat with pleasure and joy? Describe it in detail.

_____
_____
_____

_____
_____
_____
_____
_____
_____

Question 10: What's your scent?

Write down what the future version of you smells like. Maybe it's the scent of your favorite perfume or the smell of vanilla, coffee, rain, flowers, or the scent of the sea. Think and define your favorite scent. This scent should inspire you.

_____
_____
_____
_____
_____
_____
_____
_____
_____

Question 11: Where do you travel?

Where and how do you travel? Do you fly on a private jet, business class, or economy? What places do you visit, whom do you travel with, what type of hotels do you stay at, and what type of transport do you use? Is comfort important to you when traveling or do you like to travel with a backpack?

_____
_____
_____
_____
_____
_____
_____
_____

Question 12: Where does he/she invest?

Where do you invest your money? Real estate, cryptocurrencies, promising projects, startups?

_____
_____

Question 13: How do you approach conflicts?

How do you act during conflicts or unpleasant situations? Are you calm or are you irritable? What do you think about unpleasant situations? Do you take it as an opportunity? Do you react calmly, knowing that everything happens for the best and that you can handle it?

Question 14: What legacy will you leave behind for your family?

What will you leave behind for your children and relatives? Is it debt or wealth? Wisdom? A business? A conscious lifestyle?

_____
_____
_____
_____
_____
_____
_____
_____
_____

Question 15: When your future self looks back at life, what is he/she proud of?

When looking back, the future version of you says: "I'm so proud of myself for..."? It could be taking the time to work on your mindset, because this is what led you to success, for example.

What does your future self thank you for and what is that version of you proud of? Is it that you changed your job or quit and started a business? Or that you made the right choice when you invested in a project, moved to another country or city, and found the courage to change your life? Think about the things your future self will thank you for and what he/she will definitely be proud of.

_____
_____
_____
_____
_____
_____
_____
_____
_____

Question 16: What values are most important to your future self?

For example, freedom. Freedom to live where you want, freedom to move, freedom to make decisions? Honesty, awareness, generosity?

What this future version of you values the most, answer yourself with complete honesty.

_____
_____
_____
_____
_____
_____
_____
_____
_____

Question 17: What standards will he/she stand by no matter what?

This means, what will you always say and do? For example, no matter what happens, you will always try to be mindful, even if something upsets you, first you will calm down and organize your thoughts. Any decisions you make today should be consistent with this future version of you.

_____
_____

Question 18: What do others think of you?

What do other people think of this future version of you? What kind of person do you think you are? What makes you different? Write down how you would like people to think of you.

Why is this exercise so important?

Because if you don't know what the future ideal version of you is like, how can you become that person?

If you want to manifest your dream life, you need to start creating that life now! To do that, you need to behave as if you are already living that dream life in the present. And to do that, you need to know how the future version of yourself would behave.

It is also helpful to refer to your future self every time you need to make a decision. What would she/he do? With every decision, you will get closer and closer to that perfect future version of you and your dream life.

While writing out the future version of you don't use any negatives (I am not, I don't, etc.) and write in the present tense (I am, I am doing instead of I will be, I will do).

My 8 Principles of Life

1. Be curious about life. Don't aim to try everything out there but try to learn more about the things that spark your interest. Give yourself permission to do the things you enjoy. This will help you find your true calling. Be curious about yourself, explore yourself. By exploring yourself you'll be able to find answers about people and life in general. Curiosity led me to start an e-commerce business back in 2018 and through this process, I unleashed my potential. Curiosity led me to explore the topic of mindset and spirituality, which resulted in me writing this book and starting a business in this niche.

2. Savour the present moment. Our thoughts are always traveling either back to the past or forward into the future. We must learn to bring ourselves back into the present moment. Because the past is just a memory, and the future is all about our expectations. Thus, being in the present moment is the only time we are truly alive. Start pulling yourself from the past or

the future into the present moment. One way to do that is through meditation. Meditation helps stay calm and mindful which in turn leads to living life fully. Only when you're in the present moment can you truly be happy.

3. Have lots of fun. Do the things you love and not the things you have to. Even if you don't like doing a certain type of task, try to find a part of it that you actually enjoy. For instance, if you're a salesperson and you hate your job because your work consists of putting together reports and excel sheets, try to find one thing in your work that you might enjoy. In this example, it could be that you enjoy connecting with people. You can still have fun at a job you hate once you change your perspective.

Spend more time with loved ones. Do more of what lights your soul.

Do what you love and even if you fail, at least you had fun. Here's the thing, if you do what you love, eventually, you'll succeed, and more importantly you'll be happy doing what brings you joy.

4. Trust your inner voice. There will be plenty of situations and events in your life where people will try to help you or give advice. It's great to have people around you who could really help but it's best to trust your inner voice and your intuition. It's time to learn to hear your inner voice. Remember, it always whispers, and it always points to the truth. Meditations, mindfulness practices, yoga, and other spiritual activities can help you hear the voice within. By trusting your intuition, you become more conscious. You must loosen your grip, trust yourself and trust the Universe. You will always be guided and you will always make the right decisions.

5. Be audacious when it comes to your dreams. If you want to start a business, just do it. If you want to relocate, go ahead. You and only you are responsible for every aspect of your life. Be audacious enough to make a choice. Your parents, the system, friends, religion, and mass media will try to dictate the right way of living. Sometimes it's not done to harm you, they sincerely want the best for you. But consider

that they may be wrong. Because they can't know what your soul wants. So, stand up for your beliefs. Be audacious enough to say "no". This will always lead you in the right direction.

Whenever I refuse to accept something mediocre, I'm always rewarded with something better. For instance, because I said "no" to certain people, circumstances, and events, I am now where I am meant to be. I am not just an entrepreneur and owner of a business, I am the director of my own movie - my life.

6. Be grateful. Never take anything in life for granted. Be grateful for everything and everyone in your life. Be grateful for the chance to live this life. Be grateful for your soul, your body, and your mind. Even on a bad day, find something to be grateful for, for example, the opportunity to learn something from this "bad" experience. I started expressing gratitude even when it seemed like everything was going wrong. This played a huge role in helping me achieve my goals and create the life I'm living today.

7. Always keep going. In other words, never give up. If you truly want something, then you have to get it. If you feel like it belongs to you then it's already yours. You just need to keep moving. At some point in my life, I felt that I have to start my own business to fulfill my potential. So I quit my job and started something on my own and on this path I failed many times. But I always kept going and now I am an entrepreneur, author, and speaker.

8. Love yourself. It doesn't matter what you do or where you are or what is happening around you or in the world, remember to always take care of yourself. You are the only person who will always be with you no matter what. You should always treat yourself as a priority.

I got into the habit of waking up early and meditating – things I do to keep my mind calm and conscious. I eat healthy food and work out – this is for my body. I go to the beach, play chess, tennis, and paint – all for my soul. I love cheering myself up through words of affirmation and I genuinely love hugging myself.

You will never have regrets and life will always reward you if you follow these simple principles.

My wish for all of you is to passionately fall in love with this never-ending journey called life.

Epilogue

You are the master of your life. We come to Earth to discover our calling. The meaning of life has been revealed - to live life in a way that brings joy and fulfillment to the soul. And you will definitely feel this once it happens. The formula 25A + 50 + 25B will help you discover yourself, your true purpose, and the reason you're here on Earth.

Now that you know the 25A + 50 + 25B formula, you no longer have to fight to win and you can effortlessly receive what belongs to you. You can now win without defeating others. Your greatest victory is the victory over yourself. You can win without the fight, without resistance, if only you follow the voice of your soul, if only you allow yourself to hear it. Start applying this formula and I guarantee you that positive changes in your life won't keep you waiting long.

Acknowledgments

I want to thank my wife Firuza, my most faithful friend, and my love, I owe you everything. You believed in me from the very first day that we met and always supported me, no matter what. Everything that I have is thanks to your support and faith in me. You encourage and guide me, you believe in me, and share your love, warmth, care, and affection with me. I would have had a very hard time without you. You gave me strength during the most difficult times of our lives, you never lost faith. In my lowest moments, when I thought that I couldn't go on anymore, you showed me that we can achieve anything if we stick together.

Indeed, together everything is much easier. No matter how many times we fell, we always got up. We have managed to turn our world into a warm and safe place thanks to inner work.

You edited the text of this book with me several times until we realized that the book was ready for publication. Thank you for reading all the texts numerous times and giving your recommendations, as well as working on the translation of the book.

I also want to thank my grandmother Sumara, who raised me. She did everything possible and impossible for me.

Made in the USA
Middletown, DE
08 February 2023